FIRST Car
SMARTS

Daniel E. Harmon

ROSEN
PUBLISHING

New York

Published in 2010 by The Rosen Publishing Group, Inc.
29 East 21st Street, New York, NY 10010

Library of Congress Cataloging-in-Publication Data

Harmon, Daniel E.
First car smarts / Daniel E. Harmon.
    p. cm.—(Get smart with your money)
Includes bibliographical references and index.
ISBN-13: 978-1-4358-5269-3 (library binding)
ISBN-13: 978-1-4358-5544-1 (pbk)
ISBN-13: 978-1-4358-5545-8 (6 pack)
1. Automobiles—Purchasing. I. Title.
TL162.H327 2010
629.222—dc22

                                                    2008049324

Manufactured in Malaysia

Contents

Introduction

A car is expensive—a lot more expensive than you might expect. The sticker price is only the beginning of what you will have to pay. There is the endless cost of driving it (gasoline). There is the cost of keeping it running (maintenance and repairs). You will need new tires every 20,000 to 40,000 miles (32,186 to 64,372 kilometers). If you keep the car long enough, then other parts will have to be replaced, such as the exhaust system and the brakes. You must pay taxes on the car to your local government each year, and you will need to buy an insurance policy. Even with insurance, if the car is involved in an accident or is damaged by weather, then you probably will have to pay part of the repair costs.

For these reasons, some people cannot afford a car. Teenagers usually require help from their parents to buy their first car, unless they save most of their earnings from a steady part-time job for several years. Even with their parents' support, smart young buyers should examine their money math very carefully before investing in a car. They must be certain that they can earn enough to keep the car going, in addition to the purchase price.

A customer examines a car's sticker information. The price you negotiate to buy the car is only one of the costs you should expect with car ownership.

After preparing a car budget, they can decide whether or not the overall cost will be worth it. Is the car something that they really need now? Can it wait, perhaps until they are out of high school or college and have a full-time job?

When you decide it's time for your first car, a thoughtfully prepared, honest car cost worksheet will reveal what kind of vehicle you can (or can't) afford.

CHAPTER 1

"What Will My Car Really Cost?"

If you have the car-buying bug, then you are tempted everywhere you turn. There are car advertisements and classified ads in your local newspaper and on television. Banner displays beckon at the roadside wherever you pass an automobile dealership or used car lot. Friends, relatives, and neighbors often have cars to sell.

Many of the deals seem incredible. If you're a teenager with income from a part-time job and you understand the basics about budgeting and "smart money," then it may seem that you surely can afford to buy a car—now.

Maybe you can. Read beyond the advertisements, though. A young car buyer must itemize all the costs that will be involved. The advertised (purchase) price is just the beginning.

What Is the Actual Price of the Car?

You will find more than one descriptive pricing sticker on the window of a new car. A used car may carry one or more. The numbers are different. Why?

A new car may have as many as three window stickers detailing the vehicle's features and price breakdown. A buyer needs to understand what each item means.

The Invoice Price. This is the amount that the auto manufacturer charges the auto dealer. In order to make money, the car dealer must charge the customer more than this. The invoice price is basically just for your information.

The Monroney Sticker. Federal law requires that this information sheet be displayed on a window of every new vehicle sold in the United States. (It isn't required on used vehicles.) It lists the car or truck's standard and optional equipment, engine and transmission types, and estimated gas mileage (or kilometrage). (Mileage, or fuel economy, estimates are rated by the Environmental Protection Agency, or EPA.) The sticker shows the manufacturer's suggested retail price (often noted as the "MSRP") and the cost of each optional feature. It also provides warranty information.

The Sticker Price. The auto dealer attaches a separate window sticker below or beside the Monroney sticker. This is the actual price that the dealer is asking for the car. It usually is higher than the MSRP because it includes extras the dealer has provided, such as paint protection. In most cases, you can get the seller to lower the advertised price of the car.

While you consider the various stickers, you might find yourself overwhelmed by quick-sell marketing techniques. Auto dealers have always been regarded as high-powered salespeople. Many dealers offer what appear to be unbelievable terms. Examples are no down payment, no monthly payments due for six months or a year, and no problems with customers' bad credit histories.

You are led to believe that you can walk into the dealership with no money at all in your pockets, drive out in a nice (possibly brand-new) car, and pay nothing for a long time to come. Just remember the old saying, "If it seems too good to be true, then it probably is." What those dealers don't reveal until you sit down with them to talk terms is that, sooner or later, you're going to have to pay in full—and then some. Once you begin making payments, you'll likely end up paying more for the car than you would have under less fantastic but more sensible circumstances.

To begin with, they are offering only certain cars under those delayed-payment terms. In many cases, you do need a good credit record in order to qualify. Your interest rate for the car loan may be much higher than you expect (or can get, if you shop around). Overall, the terms may be far less desirable than the terms that you can easily find elsewhere. For example, the seller might require you to buy an extended service contract or special features.

Always remember that car dealers have to earn a living. They have no cars to give away, and they cannot sell them to you for less than they paid for them.

Taxes, Insurance, Etc.

Sales tax on a car is based on your state or county's tax structure. If you buy a $20,000 car and the sales tax in your area is 5 percent, then that will be an extra $1,000 ($20,000 x .05 = $1,000). It's just the beginning of taxes that you will have to pay over time. Your car will be taxable property for as long as

Shop for Insurance

Auto insurance companies offer policies with a confusing array of terms and prices. Some cover almost every eventuality. Others cover only the basics; when an accident occurs, the insurers look for ways to avoid paying. Most policies require the owner to pay a deductible for damages. That means the car owner must directly pay a certain amount—usually, the first few hundred dollars—for any repair. Only then does the insurer take over the costs.

Shopping for the best auto insurance policy is an ongoing challenge for drivers. You should review and compare your coverage every few years.

you own it. Property taxes on a car can amount to $500 or more each year. Taxes go down from year to year as the car's value decreases. Bear in mind, though, that sales and property taxes eventually add up to thousands of dollars.

Most states require car owners to buy auto insurance. The two main types of car insurance are collision and liability. Collision insurance covers damages to your car caused by your own error. Liability insurance pays others who are victims of your driving mistakes. It includes vehicle damage and medical costs.

Some states require a driver to have only liability insurance in order to obtain a driver's license. According to most advisers,

Drivers involved in a "fender bender" discuss the damages. Different types of auto insurance cover different kinds of events and repairs.

you really need more insurance than that. You can also buy comprehensive coverage (to include theft and damage by fire, vandalism, and other causes) and uninsured motorist protection. The latter will help fix your car if it is damaged by a driver who has no insurance.

Young drivers generally must pay much more for auto insurance than older drivers because statistics show that they're involved in more accidents. In some states, teenage drivers can get lower insurance rates if they pass driver training courses. If they are charged with a traffic violation or they cause an accident, then their insurance rates will most likely increase.

The car dealer may add post-sale fees for performing tasks like inspecting the vehicle, filing paperwork with the highway department, and "protecting" the paint job with a rustproof coating. Ask for explanations of every sales detail before you sign a purchase agreement.

Those are the immediate costs of buying a car. There will be ongoing costs. Besides the monthly payments and upkeep expenses, unexpected repairs are inevitable. And a sad reality is that your car begins to lose value the moment you sign the papers and drive off in it.

Myths and Facts

Myth   The least expensive car is the best deal. When it starts to have serious problems, just trade it for another cheap car.

Fact   That cheap car may get poor fuel efficiency and may require more frequent and more expensive routine maintenance. It may cost more to insure. Its resale value will be less than that of a more reliable car.

Myth   Distance driven is the most important factor to consider when buying a used car. The less distance driven, the better.

Fact   Distance driven is an important indicator, but it's not necessarily the most important. Pre-owned vehicles that have been driven responsibly for about 120,000 miles (about 200,000 km) may be capable of running another 100,000 miles (about 160,000 km) or more without needing major repairs. Any car that has been damaged or driven abusively can be a very bad deal.

Myth   If the dealer reduces the price to only a few hundred dollars "above invoice," then I'm getting a terrific deal.

Fact   In some situations it is a great deal, but not always. There are reasons why the dealer is willing to sell the car at a low markup. The model may be selling poorly or is about to be discontinued. It may have a poor maintenance record. The dealer may receive a rebate amounting to thousands of dollars from the automaker after the sale.

Chapter 2
Finding the Best Car for You

After careful planning, you have decided that you can afford to buy (and maintain) a car. You've pored through newspaper advertisements for months. Although you're still confused by some of the pros and cons of different classes of cars, you believe you are ready to proceed. Most important, you have carefully established your budget. Buying a car will mean that you can put less (or nothing) into your savings account, but it may be worth the sacrifice. If you do buy a car, then you understand what price range you can afford.

Congratulations! Now, it's time to go shopping.

You might start by visiting the Consumers Union's Web site (http://www.consumerreports.org). It reports details about specific vehicles. It also publishes comparisons and calculations on the cost, over time, of owning certain vehicles.

The Council of Better Business Bureaus' Web site (www.bbb.org) is another good resource. You can find tips on buying cars online, buying new and used cars, buying car insurance, service contracts, and more.

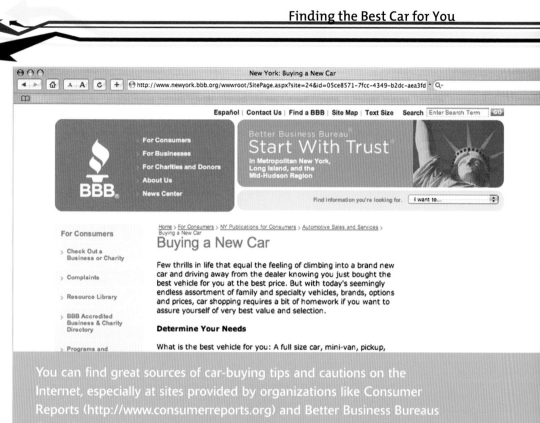

You can find great sources of car-buying tips and cautions on the Internet, especially at sites provided by organizations like Consumer Reports (http://www.consumerreports.org) and Better Business Bureaus (http://www.bbb.org).

Immerse yourself in auto advertisements. Study the details, even for cars that do not interest you. Visit local car dealerships and explore their offerings. Examine the prices and features of different cars. (Make it clear to approaching sales professionals that you are in no position to buy a car at the moment. You are gathering information.)

Car Categories

Car classifications can be confusing. There are minicars, superminis, subcompacts, compacts, and "family cars." You can investigate cabriolets, hatchbacks, sports cars, sedans, station wagons, multipurpose vehicles (MPVs), and sport utility vehicles (SUVs). You should look at all of them and decide which will best suit your purposes.

What do you need for transportation? Where do you frequently go? Do you often travel with others? How many at a time?

For most teenage car buyers, a compact car or small family car works nicely. But while compact, economical cars clearly are practical, certain factors may lead you to buy a very different vehicle type. Some parents want their teen children to drive SUVs, for example, because drivers of those cars generally are better protected in collisions than drivers of compact cars. Safety is more important to them than fuel economy.

Fuel Efficiency: A Big Factor

The sales sticker on the window will indicate the new car's expected gas mileage (or kilometrage) for city and highway driving. Vehicles get less efficiency in city driving and heavy rush-hour traffic because of frequent starts and stops. It takes extra fuel each time you accelerate the car. On the open road, you can maintain a steady speed. Energy experts advise motorists to drive as if a delicate eggshell is beneath the accelerator pedal. Avoid crushing the eggshell because pressing the accelerator burns more gas.

Once you own a car, calculating your actual fuel efficiency is simple. Step 1: Fill up the gas tank and note your current odometer reading. Step 2: Next time you fill up the gas tank, note how many gallons (or liters) it takes. Also note your new odometer reading. Step 3: Subtract the previous miles (kilometers) from the current reading. Divide that number by the number of gallons (liters) it took to refill the gasoline tank.

Example: You've driven 300 miles (482.7 km) since last filling your tank, and it takes 15 gallons (56.8 L) of gas to refill. Divide 300 by 15 (or 482.7 km by 56.8 L). You're getting 20 miles to a gallon (8.5 km to a liter) of gas. (Not good—either for the pocketbook or for the environment.)

Much nicer example: You've driven 400 miles (643.6 km) and it takes 10 gallons (37.9 L) to refill your tank. Divide 400 by 10 (or 643.6 km by 37.9 L). You're getting 40 miles to a gallon (17 km to a liter) of gas!

Until you actually own the car and make those calculations repeatedly over time, you can't know exactly how fuel-efficient the car is going to be.

Should You Buy New or Used?

Some veteran consumers never buy used cars. Others always do. Their thinking runs something like the following:

New: "If I buy a new car and trade it in two or three years (within its warranty period), I'm unlikely to ever face major

A used car can be a great deal, but you need to understand potential problems. An experienced adult who accompanies you will know what to look for and what issues to discuss with the dealer.

repair expenses. If I follow this policy for the rest of my life, I'll always enjoy relatively new, problem-free cars."

One main drawback is that you'll be making car payments constantly for the rest of your life. If you can afford that, then it's basically a sound car-buying philosophy.

Used: "If I research carefully, I can buy a very good used car that's only a couple of years old, with low mileage (kilometrage), for much less than a new model of the same car. I'll enjoy it just as much as a driver of the newer model and pay much less— both for the purchase and for property taxes."

What Is the *Blue Book*?

You may have heard the term "blue book value" in car trading. The *Kelley Blue Book* has been a trusted automobile valuation resource for many years.

When it is time to buy, sell, or trade your car, it's good to know approximately how much it is worth at current market values. The *Kelley Blue Book* is the standard resource for valuing a new or used car. You can perform an online evaluation for free at www.kbb.com. Enter the car's year, make, model, odometer reading, estimated condition, and your zip code in the United States or postal code in Canada (where you live affects car values). Check off specific features. The *Blue Book* then shows you the car's trade-in value (the amount of discount you should expect to receive from a dealer if you trade it for another car), private party value (what the car is worth if it is bought or sold by private individuals), and suggested retail value (the price at which the car dealer will probably sell the car after trading with you).

Kelley's Perfect Car Finder is an Internet tool that lets you search for car models by price range, vehicle type, category, manufacturer, seating capacity, estimated fuel economy, and size.

That may be a better idea than "staying new." But you have to know exactly what you're buying (examine the car carefully and test-drive it). You also need to possess an instinct for when it's time to trade. Generally, repair costs will mount as a car ages.

Buying an old car can be risky, and it may no longer be under warranty. Don't buy someone else's problems.

What About Leasing?

Leasing seems to cost less per month than buying, if the advertisements are to be believed. And what a car you can get! It's not only new—it's a very nice car. Think executive.

If you're an executive, a car lease might make sense. If you aren't an executive, think twice.

A leasing company will probably require a client to be twenty-one years old. You, the client, must buy insurance, perhaps more insurance than you would need if you actually owned the car. You are limited in the number of miles (kilometers) that you can drive in a year. If you go over, you pay extra. If you decide after a few months or a year that you don't like your lease agreement, it will cost you extra just to get out of it.

At the end of the lease period, you can turn in the car or buy it (usually not at a bargain price). If you don't buy it, then you own nothing. You have enjoyed day-to-day driving but have made no investment. A car owner, by contrast, still has a drivable, sellable product.

Do Your Homework

If you're a money-smart car shopper, you will spend many hours over a period of weeks or months reading car reviews and comparisons. Ask friends what they like and dislike about the cars that they drive. Visit auto dealerships in your area. If test-drives are allowed, take them. Constantly ask questions.

Chapter 3

Making the Deal

Once you've found the car you want, your objective is to buy it under the best terms that you can make. It is essential not to commit to a monthly car payment that is higher than your budget can stand. All too often, salespeople persuade buyers to pay more than they intended for a car—more than they can afford.

Negotiating with the Dealer

Car dealers buy new cars from the manufacturer for a certain price and then sell them to customers at a higher price. That is how dealers earn a profit. The more they can get above what they pay the manufacturer, the higher their profit. Dealers want all customers to think that they've gotten a great deal, regardless of the price they negotiate.

The manufacturer charges its dealers what is called the invoice price. One way that dealers attract customers is to advertise that they are selling vehicles for only a fraction "above invoice" (the amount they paid the manufacturer) or even "below invoice." They can do this and still earn a profit because they often receive money back

Dealers have ways of making profits even when it appears they're selling cars at a loss. Study the fine print, ask questions, and remember that dealers have to earn money.

from manufacturers if certain car models are not selling well. The money that the automaker pays back to the dealer is called a rebate. In some instances, the manufacturer actually charges the dealer less than the manufacturer's own invoice price. This price reduction is called a discount.

Buyers can truly get deals on vehicles that haven't been selling. Bear in mind, though, that there are good reasons why few people want to buy them. Those models may have a poor maintenance record, they may get low fuel economy, or they may hold unusually low resale values.

Pay careful attention to the details of the different stickers. Example: The manufacturer's invoice lists all the costs that the dealer has paid to the manufacturer, including freight—the charge for transporting the car from the factory to the dealership (also known as the destination or delivery charge). Some dealers have been known to add freight fees to their sticker prices. If you don't catch it, then you will pay twice for shipment.

It's wise to have an adult adviser with you when you negotiate to buy a car. Once you are pleased with the terms and the car is within your budget, some trading smarts might save you hundreds or even thousands of dollars. Never jump at the seller's first offer. If you truly believe you can get a better deal elsewhere, then tell the dealer.

When buying a used car, the original invoice price will mean little. What you want to know before sitting down to bargain with the seller is the car's blue book value. You also need to obtain as many details as you can about the history of the car. Was it wrecked? (If so, then how many times? To what extent?) Was it washed over in a flood? Has it been repaired with cheap replacement parts? If so, then those non-factory parts—especially in the emissions system—can damage related parts. Substandard replacement parts can make a warranty legally worthless.

Warranties and Service Contracts

New cars and some used cars are sold under warranty. That means if certain parts break or act up during the first few years of ownership, then the dealer or manufacturer must fix the car for free. Some warranties are more useful than others. Some fail to cover certain types of problems or parts. If a dealer promises bumper-to-bumper coverage, then you would think that means the warranty will pay for anything that goes wrong with the car. But many so-called bumper-to-bumper warranties exclude some items.

Dealers frequently try to persuade customers to pay extra for an extended warranty or a separate service contract. This, they explain, will cover additional risks not covered under the manufacturer's standard warranty. It may add more time or driving miles (kilometers) to the life of the original warranty.

Some car dealers (including used car dealers) offer warranties for the "life" of the car, with "unlimited miles" and "unlimited time" for certain vehicles. Read the fine print. No seller is honestly willing to perform all future repairs at no charge until the wheels fall off the car. It's a sales device.

Getting a Loan

Ideally, the purchaser has enough money on hand to pay for the car in full. That requires years of careful savings. Most buyers must obtain a loan in order to purchase a car. This lets them pay for the car over a period of years, during which time they can use and enjoy the vehicle. Loans cost money. Depending on the terms of the loan, the person usually

You can never ask too many questions when negotiating to buy a car. Issues to consider include details not only about the car but also about warranties and loan conditions.

pays several thousand dollars more for the car than the negotiated price.

The buyer must pay at least a small amount of the agreed-upon price up front. This is called the down payment. (With later car purchases, the dealer may accept a trade-in vehicle as the down payment.) A bank or mortgage company will loan the buyer money to pay the remainder of the purchase cost. (Actually, the bank buys the car from the dealer. The customer then buys it from the bank.) Some car dealerships have their own lending companies.

The bank or finance company makes money by charging the customer interest on the loan. The customer eventually must pay the bank the purchase price plus the interest fee.

Car dealers usually offer incentives like reduced prices, excellent loan rates, and low down payments. Be sure you understand the full meaning of each term.

Interest rates on car loans vary widely, from 1 or 2 percent to higher than 10 percent. Usually, the more money you can put down, the lower the interest rate you can get.

A computer amortization program can calculate the exact amount that you will have to pay back. The loan payback depends on three factors: 1) the amount of money borrowed after making the down payment, 2) the annual percentage rate of the loan, and 3) the payback period.

Do You Need More Coverage?

A factory warranty may cover major repairs for the first three years or 50,000 miles (80,465 km), whichever is reached first. An extended warranty or service contract might lengthen coverage to the first six years or 100,000 miles (160,930 km). It might also promise to cover problems that are not included under the regular warranty.

Automotive experts and many consumers are leery of extended service contracts. They believe the extra coverage is not worth the cost. Car owners frequently discover that when a problem arises, the service contract doesn't cover it. Some contracts exclude certain types of repairs. They might require that the car owner pay the first $100, $200, $500, or even more of any repair fee. This means that for fairly inexpensive repairs, the owner has to pay the entire cost.

Before buying a service contract, read the fine print and ask questions. Make sure that you understand exactly what the agreement does and doesn't include.

As a simple example, suppose you agree to pay $18,000 for your car and you are able to pay the dealer $3,000 down. That means you must borrow $15,000. You find a lending institution that will loan you that amount at an annual interest rate of 10 percent. Ten percent of $15,000 equals $1,500 per year.

The good news is that you must pay interest only on the ongoing principal amount of the loan. With each monthly payment, you reduce the remaining principal amount. A portion of each payment is applied toward the principal; a smaller portion is interest. Every month, a slightly higher portion goes toward principal and a lower portion goes toward interest.

Obviously, the sooner you can pay off the loan, the less you will have to pay in interest. The only good reason to negotiate a longer loan period is that you'll have more easily affordable monthly payments. For most car buyers, the key decision is how much they can afford to pay for a car each month.

An amortization program reveals how much your monthly payments will be. It also shows, month by month, how much of your money is going to principal and how much to interest. It keeps track of the total amount you have paid in principal and interest at any given point during the loan period. At the end, you can see how much in interest the loan has cost you.

If you sign a $15,000 loan contract at a 10 percent interest rate and you commit to pay it off in three years, then your monthly payments will be about $484. At the end, you will have paid $2,424 in interest. That, added to the $18,000 purchase price (your $3,000 down, plus $15,000 borrowed), means the car has cost you $20,424.

If you take four years to pay off the car loan, then you will have to pay only $380 per month, but the total interest will be $3,023. The car will have cost you $21,023. If you take five

It's wise to take an adult with you when you shop for a car. In fact, you will probably need a parent's financial help to make the purchase.

years to pay off your loan, then your monthly payment comes down to about $319 and your total interest goes up to $3,380. The car will have cost you $21,380.

As you can see, you will save almost $1,000 if you can make the monthly payments for a three-year loan, rather than a five-year loan. You'll also be free of the burden of car payments two years sooner—a very nice stress relief, as longtime car owners well know. With most loans, you can pay extra in months when you have more money available. This might shorten the loan term and save some of the interest costs.

It's hard for a high school student to qualify for a car loan, even a student who has a steady part-time job. You may need your parents to obtain the loan for you. They may expect you to make the full monthly payments, or a big part.

One final tip: If a car dealer requires you to take out a loan through its in-house or preferred lending institution, walk away from the deal. Many other banks and credit unions are available.

Chapter 4

The Power Question

Autumn 1973 was a stressful and uncertain time for Americans, especially those who had to drive every day. During the previous half century, the nation had become largely dependent on cars and trucks for transportation—vehicles powered by gasoline. Suddenly, there was a huge problem: a shortage of gasoline. The 1973 fuel crisis came on quickly, without warning.

What caused it was a brief war in the Middle East. Israel, a Jewish nation, was fighting against two Muslim nations, Egypt and Syria. The Organization of Petroleum Exporting Countries (OPEC) is a league of twelve oil-producing nations, most of them Muslim-controlled. OPEC voted to stop exporting oil to Western countries that supported Israel. Within days, gas stations in the United States and other countries began running out of gas. Cars and trucks lined up at the stations that did have gas. Station owners began rationing their supplies, limiting customers to only $5 or $10 worth of gas at a time. Other rationing systems were devised. In some areas, drivers could buy gas only on odd or even days, determined by their license plate numbers.

Traffic jams at filling stations were a common scene during the autumn 1973 gasoline shortage. Less serious shortages since then have continued to remind Americans that fuel resources are limited.

The good thing about the 1973 fuel crisis was that it made drivers think about energy and ways to conserve gasoline. Sadly, after the crisis passed, most drivers went back to their old, wasteful consumption of gasoline.

The United States has not experienced another energy shortage that serious. There have been local and regional gas shortages, though. Hurricanes damaged oil rigs in the Gulf of Mexico in 2008. This resulted in temporary shortages of gasoline to southeastern states. Again, lines formed at gas stations and backed up into the streets. Fights, even shootings and knife attacks, broke out at gas pumps.

These events, coupled with environmental awareness, have led many people to seek alternative forms of transportation. The use of fossil fuels, including gasoline, contributes to pollution. Consumers are interested in fuel types that are not subject to unpredictable, faraway developments. They are also interested in power sources that will cause less damage to the environment.

Gasoline-Powered Autos

The great majority of cars are fueled by gasoline. Auto engineers, scientists, government officials, consumer groups, and experimental individuals endeavor to find better alternatives. For the near future, however, most of your choices will be gas-powered autos.

If you buy a gas-powered car, then you become the typical customer at the pump. Your car budget will be affected by price trends and crises in petroleum production and supply. When prices rise or when supplies are limited, you can only grumble and bear it—and look for ways to conserve on gas.

One pump choice you do have is the fuel grade you will use. When you pull up to a gas pump, you find at least two, usually

Regular, mid-grade, or premium—which grade of gasoline should you run in your car? Advisers disagree on whether or not higher grades are worth the higher prices.

three, choices: regular, mid-grade, and premium. The differences in price are about 10 cents per gallon (13 cents per liter). What is the advantage of paying more for higher gasoline grades?

Most cars run fine on the cheapest grade, regular. Some cars, such as sports cars, have engines that function best on higher gas grades. These are called high-performance cars. They will run on regular gasoline, but their engines might begin to knock or "ping." Some advisers say the engine noise is barely noticeable and is basically harmless. Others say using the wrong gas grade can damage an engine. A good rule of thumb is to read consumer accounts and ask the car dealer.

Conservation Tips

Even after you buy your car, don't drive if you can walk or bike instead. This advice applies with any car you buy, regardless of its power supply or fuel/mileage economy rating.

Carpool whenever possible. Share a ride to that distant concert or sports event with friends. (It would be nice if they would buy the gas, since you're providing the car.)

Combine errands. When you can, combine business with pleasure, too. If you would like to check out the new seasonal clothes at the mall and you have library books due, and the library is between your home and the mall, make one trip. If you want to make a bank deposit and your bank is on the way to your job, stop by the bank on your way to or from work.

Remember that the faster you drive, the more gas you consume.

Saving Gas = Saving Money

It's wonderful to have your own car! You're proud and free. Financial experts, though, put a damper on the excitement. They advise that you drive it only when necessary.

First-time car owners have a hard time abiding by that. They've already planned fun trips. They want to show off their "wheels" to friends. They would like to drive around the town and countryside, enjoying that special scent of a new car's interior and the feeling of power.

It's OK to enjoy your car, but money-smart drivers understand the need for discipline. They always count the cost in advance. If you want to drive to a concert or sporting event that is in a distant city, calculate the round-trip mileage (kilometrage). Depending on your car's fuel economy and current pump prices, a 100-mile (160-km) trip could cost you $15 to $20 just for the gasoline.

Alternatives to Gasoline

Gas-powered vehicles are the most common. There are two major reasons to consider buying a car powered by a different fuel type.

First, fossil fuels like petroleum (the source of our gas and oil) won't last forever. They were made naturally over a period of millions of years. They came from the earth, and the supply is limited. When they are all used up, that will be the end of the fossil fuel story. Scientists can only speculate how much more fossil fuel is available. The supply will probably last longer than your lifetime, but it will be gone eventually.

Second, the burning of fossil fuels produces carbon dioxide and badly pollutes the earth's atmosphere. Experimenters have proven that other types of automotive power cause less atmospheric damage—practically no damage, in some cases.

Money is a factor. In general, cars that run with alternative energy are more expensive. The purchase price almost certainly will be higher than that for a gas-powered vehicle. After the purchase, the fuel/energy supply may or may not cost you more to keep the car on the road. You can find out many of the details by researching in advance. You should ask the car seller about the long-term economics of the deal.

You might conclude that it's important to invest in an alternative-powered car for the sake of the environment, even if it costs more. You may decide to buy a gas-powered car that gets excellent fuel efficiency and produces a low level of hazardous emissions. Unavoidably, some people need a vehicle type (perhaps a five-passenger, four-wheel-drive truck) that simply can't meet economic or environmental ideals.

Alternative power systems include the following:

Diesel. Diesel engines and special diesel fuel have been used since the early 1900s, notably by the military and the trucking industry. Modern diesel fuel is a petroleum (fossil fuel) product, but it costs less to produce than standard gasoline does. It has several other advantages, too. Besides being safer to handle than gasoline, it contains less sulfur, making it less polluting. For money watchers, its main asset is that it gets roughly a third better fuel efficiency than gas-powered vehicles.

Biodiesel. Scientists have found that more environmentally friendly, biologically grown fuels can be blended with traditional diesel fuel. Soybean oil is an example. Some forms of biodiesel fuel can reduce harmful exhaust by as much as two-thirds, compared to pure gasoline.

Ethanol. This is a type of alcohol brewed not for human consumption but for powering cars. It can be produced from corn and other biological ingredients, including certain waste materials.

Electric. Electric cars are available in the United States. Specialty shops can convert some gas-powered automobiles to electric power by adding batteries. Certain car designs are easier to convert than others. A major problem with electric cars is

High school students in Ohio recycle cooking oil from the school kitchen. It will be used in a project to make biodiesel fuel for school buses.

limited range. You can't drive nearly as far on an electrical battery charge as you can on a tank of gasoline. For short daily trips, though, this may be an option worth considering. You may have to recharge the battery only once every few days. Keep in mind that electrical current costs money, too.

Hybrid. A hybrid is an electrically powered vehicle that also has a gas or diesel engine. Why? The purpose of the petroleum-based system is to keep the electric batteries charged. This helps solve the problem of limited range.

Other alternatives. Natural gas can power cars efficiently. However, like petroleum, it is an earth-bound natural resource. Sooner or later, the world's supply of natural gas will be gone. Another energy source is hydrogen, but the cost of researching, developing, and marketing it is high.

If you are interested in investing in an alternatively powered vehicle, then make sure that you understand all the costs, both short-term and long-term, before you buy. It may cost you more to purchase but save you more in the long run—or it may cost more altogether. In some instances, it comes down to a decision between car economy and environmental responsibility.

CHAPTER 5
How Long Should You Keep It?

A general rule is to keep the car as long as possible after it's paid for. With no more monthly loan payments, the total cost of your car ownership becomes fairly cheap over time. Repairs are likely to increase as the car ages, however. When repairs become frequent, or when a major repair would cost you more than a sizable down payment on a new car, it's probably time to trade.

Some people trade cars every two or three years. (A few trade every year.) The main advantage for them—apart from always having a nice, new car—is that with a newer car, they're more likely to avoid the cost of major repairs.

The disadvantage is that the quick seller takes a beating on the buy/sell exchange. A car begins losing its value the moment you buy it. If you buy a new car for $20,000 and trade it three years later, then you might be offered no more than $10,000 for it—half your purchase price. Did you get your money's worth during that brief time? If you keep it for another three years, then the resale value might be reduced to $5,000. As you can see, it lost $10,000 in resale value during the first three years but only $5,000 more during

A mechanic explains needed repairs to a car owner. There comes a point in a car's life when mounting repair costs signal that it's time to trade it in for a different one.

the next three years. If you keep the car for ten years or longer, then you might receive only $1,000 for it when you finally trade. However, you'll have gotten ten years of drive time.

A car loses resale value rapidly during the first few years. Later, the rate of decreasing value levels off. The longer you keep it, the more value you will get from it.

"How Do I Recognize (and Get Rid of) a Lemon?"

A car that has a recurring problem is called a lemon. All U.S. states have lemon laws. They require automakers to replace or buy back cars that, after repeated attempts, have not been repaired satisfactorily under terms of the warranty. If you have repeated problems with your new car and the dealer is unhelpful, then you may have a case under your state's lemon law.

What about used lemons? They may not be as easy to challenge under your state's lemon law. To what extent are you protected, then, under state law? You should find out your legal options before buying a used car.

Keep Your Car in Good Condition

No matter how long you plan to keep your car, keep it in good shape. Regular maintenance will help your car last longer and avoid major repairs as it ages. It will also help keep the car's resale value as high as possible.

Repairs are inevitable. They might be as simple and inexpensive as having a punctured tire patched for $10 to $20. If

The *Kelley Blue Book* and its Web site (http://www.kbb.com) give you a good idea of what you will pay for any new or used car model, as well as how much to ask when you sell.

the tire cannot be repaired, then a new tire might cost $50 to $200. That's minor, though, compared with major car repairs. Structural and engine repairs can easily run into thousands of dollars. When faced with a repair estimate of $3,000 or more on a car with an estimated blue book value of perhaps $1,000, you have to ask yourself, "Should I keep this car?"

Meanwhile, keep the odometer in mind. The odometer reading will greatly affect your car's resale value.

No matter how well you maintain your car and how low you keep the mileage (kilometrage), the car will depreciate, or decrease in value, simply because it is getting old. When it's time to sell or trade your car, you should find out approximately how much it is worth. For used car sellers and buyers alike, the *Kelley Blue Book* is the standard pricing guide.

Ten Great Questions to Ask
A CAR DEALER

1 According to my budget, I can afford the monthly payments you're estimating for this car. I can also afford fuel, regular maintenance checkups, and insurance. What other expenses am I overlooking?

2 If I'll need for a parent to help me obtain the car loan, and I make the payments, will the car belong to my parent or to me after it's paid for?

3 I'm interested in leasing as well as in buying a car. Am I old enough to lease?

4 Are used cars that have been leased or driven in company fleets usually good buys?

5 You're asking much more for this used car than the *Blue Book* suggested price. Why?

6 Before I buy this new car, can you tell me how rapidly it's likely to decrease in value in the coming years, assuming ordinary wear?

7 Does your advertised price include sales tax?

8 How often will I need to bring in the car for servicing? What's the average maintenance charge?

9 How much should I expect to pay for a new set of tires? How many miles should I expect to get from new tires?

10 Rather than trading my old car for this new one, I'm thinking of selling the old one myself. Would it be to my advantage to trade it with you?

CHAPTER 6

Smart Cars, Cycles, Scooters, and Mopeds

Alternative transportation methods are exciting for many reasons. Today, environmental awareness is a major topic of discussion. People want to find safe ways to go wherever they want while emitting as few pollutants into the air as possible. To achieve that goal, many Americans are looking at transportation alternatives.

The following are some "non-car" options that you might want to think about. All of them will save you gas money. But be aware that all of them also pose safety risks. These vehicles are much smaller than what you normally encounter on the highway. Whenever they're involved in accidents, they almost always receive worse damage than larger vehicles.

Smart Cars

You've probably seen them: little two-seat "bug" cars. If you've seen them on an interstate highway with an eighteen-wheel truck bearing down on their bumper at 70 miles (113 km) an hour, then you probably have decided that you don't want to be inside one of them.

Smart cars are cute and fuel-efficient, getting up to 40 miles to a gallon (17 km to a liter) of gas. Drawbacks are obvious: limited seating and storage and comparative fragility, if involved in a collision.

But they serve a purpose. To rove high-speed interstate highways? Probably not. But to get around town or take jaunts on quiet back roads? Perhaps.

Smart cars have many definitions. Some call them super-minis or micro-cars. (They are also lovingly called smarties.) They can go up to 80 miles (130 km) per hour. Prices and locations vary. They may cost as little as $12,000 or as much as $30,000, depending on the features that they include. Some smart cars are electric, boasting a range of up to 70 miles (113 km) between charges.

Many observers believe smart cars are better suited for Europeans, who need to drive shorter distances than Americans do. But Americans are beginning to take notice.

Weighing the Factors

People interested in buying an alternative vehicle are attracted mainly by its economy. They also like that it pollutes the atmosphere less than conventional vehicles do. They may be impressed by the visual appeal—the "cute" look of a smart car or scooter, or the exciting designs of late-model motorcycles.

The obvious factor that turns other buyers away is the size. Only one passenger besides the driver can ride on a scooter or motorcycle or inside a smart car, and few items can be carried along. Another negative is the lack of comfort compared to roomier vehicles. Finally, mainte-nance is inconvenient if the nearest service shop is across town or in a distant city.

Some are thinking a smart car is just the kind of car they need. But smart cars are comparatively rare in the United States. You may have to get on a waiting list to buy a new one. Used smart cars are sold locally and through online auctions.

Although they are turning heads and are environmentally friendly, smart cars are not much more economical than many late-model compact cars. They can get up to 40 miles per gallon (17 km per liter) of gas.

Motorcycles, Scooters, and Mopeds

You will need a special driver's license or permit and substantial experience in order to drive a motorcycle or scooter. Motorcycle laws vary among states, in terms of vehicle classes and age requirements. (Although some states don't require it, do wear a helmet.) You can buy a new motorcycle for less than $10,000 and a good used one for around $5,000. Fuel economy? Expect to get 50 to 60 miles to a gallon (21.25 to 25.5 km per liter) of gas. You can drive 80 or 90 miles (129 or 145 km) an hour on a motorcycle if you want to flirt with death.

A motor scooter with a 150cc (cubic centimeter) engine can move you around at 60 miles (97 km) per hour or faster at an economy rating of about 80 miles per gallon (34 km per liter) of gasoline. The purchase price is under $1,500 for many Chinese-built models and more for American- and European-made scooters. You can buy scooters with 250cc or larger engines. Generally, the larger the engine, the faster you can go but the lower your gas mileage (kilometrage) will be. Some scooters can press 100 miles (160 km) per hour, but don't expect remarkable fuel economy. And you really would be wearing your life on your sleeve at that speed on a scooter.

Scooters became very popular in summer 2008, when gasoline prices averaged $4 per gallon in the United States. Depending on the engine type, fuel economy ranges from 50 to more than 100 miles per gallon (from 21.25 to 42.5 km per liter).

Scooters are designed for fairly short-distance, moderate-speed driving. Motorcycles are more controllable than scooters at higher speeds.

A moped with a 50cc engine or smaller can go only about 35 miles (56 km) per hour but can carry you more than 100 miles on a gallon (42.5 km per liter) of gas. Some high school and college students have decided that a moped is just what they need for their day-to-day transportation. You can buy a new moped for under $1,000. In many states, you don't need a motorcycle permit, license tag, or special insurance to own and drive it. But you do have to be the state's required age and pass a driver's test.

Motorcycle and scooter maintenance costs less than car maintenance does. For example, whereas an oil change for a car may require 4 quarts (3.8 L) of new oil, a two-wheel vehicle may require a quart (just under 1 L) or less.

But maintenance is a thorny issue for two-wheel motorists in some locations. It's simple to arrange an inexpensive car tune-up within easy driving distance of your home. Cycle and scooter service centers, by contrast, are not as easy to find. Many two-wheel drivers learn to do their own maintenance. This can save them lots of money if they're willing to master the details and perform the work. A do-it-yourself, two-wheel owner must be diligent in maintaining the engine, transmission, tires, brakes, battery, shock absorbers, and other parts for safety reasons.

How Safe Is an Alternative Vehicle?

It definitely is not safe if you do not know how to drive your two-wheeler or maneuver your smart car among larger vehicles in thick traffic. Highway department officials lay it out in plain language: If you are a driver or passenger aboard a cycle or

Whether you're interested in a car, truck, or alternative vehicle, your first purchase will be a more enjoyable, economical experience if you spend time in advance studying the options.

inside a micro-size car and you're involved in a collision, then you almost always will get the worst of it. The other vehicle might be a truck, an SUV, or an eighteen-wheeler.

That does not necessarily mean you should avoid alternative vehicles. It just means you must plan and understand your transportation needs very carefully. Where do you need to drive? How far? How often? Do you need a versatile first car—one that can take you around the block and carry you on long-distance journeys? Will you be jostling frequently with interstate traffic?

Smart cars are considered urban vehicles, to be driven around the city or on short trips. So are scooters. Mopeds are not intended to be driven more than a few miles at a time. Motorcycles, on the other hand, may be long-distance cruisers.

Be a Responsible Car Owner

Whether you buy a new car, used car, small car, big car, gas-powered or alternate car, or a two-wheel vehicle, you must do your homework in advance. Understand all of the costs, not just the purchase price. Be prepared to deal with unexpected expenses. Make sure that you can afford not only to buy the car but also to keep it running.

Always be mindful of ways to conserve. Transportation is often a luxury, not a necessity. The less you drive, the better off the environment will be—and the better off your budget will be.

Glossary

amortization program A computer program that calculates details of a loan.

cabriolet A two-door convertible with a small backseat.

consumer Buyer or user of a product.

deductible An amount of an insurance claim that the insured person must pay before the insurance company begins its coverage.

depreciate To lose value; except for classic vehicles, all cars depreciate over time.

discount A lowering of the stated price of an item.

down payment The amount of money a car buyer pays in cash (or by check) before taking out a loan for the remainder of the cost.

export To sell a product (such as oil) to buyers in other countries.

fossil fuel Petroleum, coal, or another type of fuel that was formed in the earth from plant or animal fossils over a long period of time.

hatchback A compact or subcompact car with a rear door that opens upward.

interest A percentage of a borrowed amount of money that must be paid to the lender or investor, in addition to the original amount.

invoice price The price that a car manufacturer charges its dealers.

kilometrage The total distance in kilometers.

maintenance Upkeep of a car.

MPV Multipurpose vehicle.

odometer The dashboard instrument that records how many miles (or kilometers) a car is driven.

optional equipment Additional features that a car buyer can purchase, such as power locks, cruise control, a built-in navigational system, etc.

petroleum Flammable oil used to prepare gasoline and other products.

principal The amount of money borrowed.

rationing A system that forces people to use products like gasoline or food sparingly.

rebate Payback of part of a purchase price to the buyer.

sedan An average-size car with a backseat and either two or four doors.

sticker price The actual asking price on a car.

SUV Sport utility vehicle.

warranty The guarantee that if certain parts of a car do not work properly, they will be repaired or replaced at no cost to the buyer.

For More Information

American Automobile Association, Inc. (AAA)
1415 Kellum Place
Garden City, NY 11530
(516) 746-7730
Web site: http://www.aaa.com
AAA is a federation of automobile clubs across the United
States and in other countries. Besides member services,
it provides consumer information like new and used
car-buying tips.

Canada Extra
Consumers Union
101 Truman Avenue
Yonkers, NY 10703-1057
(914) 378-2000
Web site: http://www.consumerreports.org/cro/
canadaextra/index.htm
At Canada Extra, you can find Canada-specific information
about cars and other products provided by
ConsumerReports.org.

Canadian Council of Better Business Bureaus
2 St. Clair Avenue East
Toronto, ON M4T 2T5
Canada
(416) 644-4936
Web site: http://www.ccbbb.ca
Among its other consumer services, the council offers buying
advice for many product categories, including used cars.
(See http://www.ccbbb.ca/cadvice_auto.cfm.)

CARFAX
Web site: http://www.carfax.com
To aid used car buyers, CARFAX, a commercial Web site,
    offers vehicle history information on car and light truck
    models made since 1981. Its databases reportedly contain
    information on more than 5 billion vehicles, identifying
    them by their vehicle identification numbers (VINs).

Cars.com
Classified Ventures, LLC
175 W. Jackson Boulevard
Chicago, IL 60604
(312) 601-5000
Web site: http://www.cars.com
A commercial Web site that provides information from experts
    and consumers to help buyers formulate opinions on what
    to buy, where to buy, and how much to pay for a car.

ConsumerReports.org
Consumers Union
101 Truman Avenue
Yonkers, NY 10703-1057
(914) 378-2000
Web site: http://www.consumerreports.org
Consumer Reports publishes information for consumers
    about thousands of products, including new and used
    car models. It reports on cars by type: convertibles,
    small cars, minivans, pickups, SUVs, sedans, wagons,
    and sports cars.

Council of Better Business Bureaus
4200 Wilson Boulevard, Suite 800

Arlington, VA 22203-1838
(703) 276-0100
Web site: http://www.bbb.org
The council's auto-related consumer services include buying
    tips and BBB AUTO LINE for resolving warranty disputes.

Edmunds.com
Web site: http://www.edmunds.com
Edmunds, Inc., has been publishing new and used auto-
    mobile pricing guidelines since 1966. Among other
    services, it operates the CarSpace network (http://
    www.carspace.com) where people share information
    about specific car models and discuss many car-
    related issues.

Federal Trade Commission (FTC)
600 Pennsylvania Avenue NW
Washington, DC 20580
(202) 326-2222
Web site: http://www.ftc.gov
The consumer information section of the FTC's Web site
    includes advice on car purchasing, leasing, and renting,
    as well as financing and maintenance.

Kelley Blue Book Co., Inc.
195 Technology
Irvine, CA 92618
(800) 258-3266
Web site: http://www.kbb.com
Long famous for its auto valuation service, the Kelley organi-
    zation also provides online advice, reviews, and other
    material for car buyers and sellers.

National Automobile Dealers Association
8400 Westpark Drive
McLean, VA 22102
(703) 821-7000
Web site: http://www.nada.org
See especially the association's "Auto Financing Resources"
page (http://www.nada.org/Advocacy+Outreach/
Auto+Financing+Resources).

National Highway Traffic Safety Administration (NHTSA)
1200 New Jersey Avenue SE
West Building
Washington, DC 20590
(888) 327-4236
Web site: http://www.nhtsa.gov
The NHTSA works to achieve the highest standards in
motor vehicle and highway safety. See the site's link
to Safercar.gov for vehicle safety information like
safety recalls, rollover prevention, tire ratings, and
airbag safety.

Web Sites

Due to the changing nature of Internet links, Rosen Publishing
has developed an online list of Web sites related to the subject
of this book. This site is updated regularly. Please use this link
to access the list:

http://www.rosenlinks.com/gsm/car

For Further Reading

Berg, Adriane, Arthur Bochner, and Rose Bochner. *The New Totally Awesome Money Book for Kids*. New York, NY: Newmarket Press, 2007.

Denega, Danielle. *Smart Money* (How to Manage Your Cash). New York, NY: Franklin Watts, 2008.

Edwards, Stephen. *50 + 1 Questions When Buying a Car*. Fox Island, WA: Encouragement Press LLC, 2006.

Fix, Lauren. *Lauren Fix's Guide to Loving Your Car: Everything You Need to Know to Take Charge of Your Car and Get On with Your Life*. New York, NY: St. Martin's Press, 2008.

Gardner, David. *The Motley Fool Investment Guide for Teens: 8 Steps to Having More Money Than Your Parents Ever Dreamed Of*. Alexandria, VA: The Motley Fool Press, 2003.

Harman, Hollis Page. *Barron's Money Sense for Kids!* 2nd ed. Hauppauge, NY: Barron's Educational Series, Inc., 2004.

Hollander, Barbara. *Managing Money*. Chicago, IL: Heinemann Publishing, 2008.

Holmberg, Joshua, and David Bruzzese. *The Teen's Guide to Personal Finance: Basic Concepts in Personal Finance That Every Teen Should Know*. Littleton, CO: iUniverse, 2008.

McGillian, Jamie Kyle. *The Kids' Money Book*. New York, NY: Sterling Publishing Co., Inc., 2003.

Munroe, Brian. *Car Buying Revealed: How to Buy a Car and Not Get Taken for a Ride*. Garden City, NY: Morgan James Publishing, 2008.

Stahl, Mike. *Early to Rise: A Young Adult's Guide to Investing and Financial Decisions That Can Shape Your Life*. Los Angeles, CA: Silver Lake Publishing, 2005.

Sutton, Remar. *Don't Get Taken Every Time: The Ultimate Guide to Buying or Leasing a Car, in the Showroom or on the Internet*. New York, NY: Penguin Group, 2007.

Bibliography

Babej, Marc E., and Tim Pollak. "Is Smart a Dumb Idea?"
    Forbes, July 12, 2006. Retrieved October 16, 2008
    (http://www.forbes.com/2006/07/12/unsolicited-advice-
    advertising-meb_0712smart.html).

ConsumerReports.org. "What That Car Really Costs to Own."
    Retrieved October 2008 (http://www.consumerreports.org/
    cro/cars/pricing/what-that-car-really-costs-to-own-4-08/
    overview/what-that-car-really-costs-to-own-ov.htm).

Council of Better Business Bureaus News Center.
    "Buying a Used Car." March 25, 2003. Retrieved
    October 18, 2008 (http://us.bbb.org/
    WWWRoot/SitePage.aspx?site=113&id=
    1869d6a9-82aa-49a1-8419-40a8251fa916&art=404).

Council of Better Business Bureaus News Center. "Know
    the Facts About Auto Service Contracts." October 30,
    2003. Retrieved October 18, 2008 (http://us.bbb.org/
    WWWRoot/SitePage.aspx?site=113&id=
    1869d6a9-82aa-49a1-8419-40a8251fa916&art=424).

Federal Trade Commission. "Buying a New Car." Facts for
    Consumers, April 2006. Retrieved October 18,
    2008 (http://www.ftc.gov/bcp/edu/pubs/consumer/
    autos/aut11.shtm).

Federal Trade Commission. "Buying a Used Car." Facts for
    Consumers, June 2008. Retrieved October 18,
    2008 (http://www.ftc.gov/bcp/edu/pubs/consumer/
    autos/aut03.shtm).

Federal Trade Commission. "Consider the Alternatives:
    Alternative Fueled Vehicles and Alternative Vehicle
    Fuels." Facts for Consumers, April 2006. Retrieved
    October 18, 2008 (http://www.ftc.gov/bcp/edu/pubs/
    consumer/autos/aut01.shtm).

Kelley Blue Book. "10 Steps to Buying a New Car." Retrieved October 2008 (http://www.kbb.com/kbb/Advice/Step.aspx?ContentUniqueName=KBBWebContent-85).

Kelley Blue Book. "10 Steps to Buying a Used Car." Retrieved October 2008 (http://www.kbb.com/kbb/Advice/Step.aspx?ContentUniqueName=KBBWebContent-97).

Kelley Blue Book. "10 Steps to Selling Your Car." Retrieved October 2008 (http://www.kbb.com/kbb/Advice/Step.aspx?ContentUniqueName=KBBWebContent-508).

The Learning Calendar. "Gas Shortage Begins." Retrieved October 14, 2008 (http://www.learningcalendar.com/this_day_in_history/days_template.cfm?history_id=60498).

Peters, Craig. "Mo-peds and Scooters Create a Debate on Wheels." *Herald-Journal* (Spartanburg, SC), October 19, 2008. Retrieved October 2008 (http://www.goupstate.com/article/20081019/NEWS/810190383).

SmartCarOfAmerica.com. "Want to Buy a Smart Car?" Retrieved October 17, 2008 (http://www.smartcarofamerica.com).

Smartusa.com. "Smart fortwo pure." Retrieved October 2008 (http://www.smartusa.com/smart-fortwo-pure.aspx).

The Straight Dope. "What's the Difference Between Premium and Regular Gas?" Retrieved October 14, 2008 (http://www.straightdope.com/columns/read/2565/whats-the-difference-between-premium-and-regular-gas).

Valdes-Dapena, Peter. "Invoice Price: What's It Really Worth?" CNNMoney.com, July 22, 2004. Retrieved October 2008 (http://money.cnn.com/2003/11/24/pf/autos/invoice_price/index.htm).

Woodyard, Chris. "America Crazy About Breadbox on Wheels Called Smart Car." *USA Today*, November 12, 2007. Retrieved October 2008 (http://www.usatoday.com/money/autos/2007-11-11-smartcar_N.htm).

Index

About the Author

Daniel E. Harmon is the author of more than sixty books and numerous articles for national and regional magazines and newspapers. In high school, he drove an aging, imported lemon, whenever it decided to start up and move. When he entered college, his mother found a terrific deal on a used compact sedan; he worked part-time and shared college and car expenses with his parents. He recently bought a 150cc motor scooter for daily errands and calculates that he saves 10 cents every mile he uses the scooter instead of the car. He lives in Spartanburg, South Carolina.

Photo Credits

Cover (foreground) © www.istockphoto.com/RickBL; cover, p. 1 (top) Scott Olson/Getty Images; cover, p. 1 (middle) © www. istockphoto.com/Sophie Ledeme-Goodman; cover, p. 1 (bottom) © www.istockphoto.com/Willie B. Thomas; pp. 4–5 © Lee White/Corbis; pp. 7, 14, 21, 31, 40, 45 © www.istockphoto.com/ Catherine Yeulet; p. 8 Scott Olson/Getty Images; p. 11 © Jim Craigmyle/Corbis; p. 18 © Nancy P. Alexander/PhotoEdit; p. 22 © Najlah Feanny/Corbis; p. 25 © Franco Vogt/Corbis; p. 26 Tim Boyle/Getty Images; p. 29 © age fotostock/SuperStock; p. 32 Allan Tannenbaum/Getty Images; p. 34 © www.istockphoto.com/ Michael Krinke; p. 38 © AP Images; p. 41 © www.istockphoto. com/Sean Locke; p. 46 © Matthew Roberts/Zuma Press; p. 49 Joe Raedle/Getty Images; p. 51 © Bob Daemmrich/ the Image Works.

Designer: Sam Zavieh; Editor: Kathy Kuhtz Campbell; Photo Researcher: Amy Feinberg